D0210282

leave your mind
behind

the everyday practice of finding

stillness amid rushing thoughts

matthew mckay, ph.d.
& catharine sutker

New Harbinger Publications, Inc.

Publisher's Note

Distributed in Canada by Raincoast Books

Copyright © 2007 by Matthew McKay & Catharine Sutker
New Harbinger Publications, Inc.
5674 Shattuck Avenue
Oakland, CA 94609
www.newharbinger.com

Cover and text design by Amy Shoup; Acquired by Tesilya Hanauer

---

Library of Congress Cataloging-in-Publication Data

McKay, Matthew.

Leave your mind behind : the everyday practice of finding stillness amid rushing thoughts / Matthew McKay and Catharine Sutker.

p. cm.

ISBN-13: 978-1-57224-534-1

ISBN-10: 1-57224-534-4

1. Thought and thinking. 2. Peace of mind. I. Sutker, Catharine. II. Title.

BF441.M425 2007

158.1--dc22

2007028149

10   09   08

10 9 8 7 6 5 4 3 2

contents

PART II: what do your thoughts do to your life?

PART III: stop believing everything you think

acknowledgments

Grateful acknowledgement to Steven C. Hayes, Ph.D., Kelly G. Wilson, Ph.D., and Kirk Strosahl, Ph.D., and the entire ACT community, for developing an extraordinary therapy-acceptance and commitment therapy. This book is based on a component of that therapy, cognitive defusion.

INTRODUCTION

the art of leaving your mind behind

When you wake, your mind starts a day's journey. It's like you're getting in a car, and your mind is driving. Sometimes it goes at breakneck speed; sometimes you can't get out of the garage. Sometimes it guides you precisely to a destination; sometimes it takes you down a road of ruts and weeds to the middle of nowhere. Your mind can show you streets with lofty houses and sloping lawns—places where you feel a sense of jealousy and failure. Or it can strand you in back alleys, full of danger and moving shadows.

For so many of us, our minds go places we wish we didn't have to follow. Our thoughts may have an automatic quality, rushing us into feelings of fear, loss, unworthiness, or anger. We get so attached to our thoughts that they seem real and drive us to do things that create even more pain. This book is about how to relax and watch your mind. About letting your mind go where it goes, but taking the trip much less seriously. You'll learn to watch the mental scenery with detachment, not belief, and with interest, not involvement. As you let go of believing everything you think, those rides with your mind will feel more safe and comfortable.

The first section of this book will introduce you to the five types of thoughts. You'll learn how to recognize and watch them; and how to switch from one kind of thought to another. In the book's second part, you'll learn to recognize the function and effects of your thoughts. When you can see through thoughts, when you know what they're designed to do or create, they have far less power over you. Section three will show you how to watch a thought without getting caught in its content. You'll learn to disengage from the scary, hurtful things thoughts throw at you.

This book will be eye-opening. We promise. It will also give you new, creative ways to take that daily journey with your mind. So let's get going.

PART I

~

what do you think?

Our mind's main job is to create thoughts. That's what minds do—constantly, relentlessly. Some thoughts make sense; some don't. Some thoughts solve problems. Some paralyze us with fear. Some help us steer our ship. Some run us aground on the shoals of self-hate.

Our thoughts are just a moment in time, existing only in the synapses of the brain. While they're less real than a sitcom, we treat them as breaking news. We believe everything we think, and that is the source of so much of our pain. There is only one way to free ourselves from the trap of believing what our minds create. We must understand how thoughts work.

Understanding the mind begins with observing the seven kinds of thoughts, and learning to differentiate one from the other. These thoughts are:

- **Observations** *about the present moment.*

- **Memories** *of past moments.*

- **Judgments** *about whether something's good or bad, right or wrong.*

- **Storytelling thoughts** *that try to explain why things happen.*

- **Future thoughts** *that develop scenarios for things that haven't yet occurred. There are three types of future thoughts:*

planning, fantasy, *and* **fortune-telling**.
More about that later.

This book will teach you how to watch your mind. As you watch, you'll discover how each kind of thought can help or hurt you. Let's get started. There's a lot to learn about your mind. The more you know, the less your mind will control your moods and your life.

— 1 —

watching now: the moving band meditation

everything you feel inside your body can be a focusing point for the present moment. Listening to your physical experience is like listening to a complex piece of music. There are major and subordinate melodies. There are themes that swell and fade away. Sensations may explode like the sudden crashing of cymbals or come on slowly like a crescendo played on an oboe.

One easy way to listen to your body and focus your attention on the experience right now is the Moving Band Meditation. Imagine a circular band of light, about three feet in diameter just above your head. In a moment, the band will begin to descend, moving slowly down your body. As it passes each point, from your forehead to your feet, try to observe your feelings in that place. Notice the quality of each sensation. Does it feel tight? Is it a dull ache? Is there a sense of pressure, or a sense of calm or release? As the band moves lower, let your attention shift to the new area it surrounds. Bring all your focus and awareness to bear on the parts of your body that lie within the band. Keep watching the band descend, in small increments, until you have listened to each sensation, each individual note of the body's song.

Now expand your awareness to include the whole melody. Inhale a deep breath and let it go; take in everything your body feels. Listen for a moment with your whole attention. Then take another deep breath and end the exercise.

Go ahead now. Start the Moving Band Meditation. The most important thing about the meditation is what you're *not* doing. For the most part, you aren't worrying, planning, remembering, explaining, or expecting. During these few moments, your mind has been quieter. It has been watching and listening. It has been living in this moment, and no other.

Think about these questions:

■   *How does focusing your mind on
    sensations, even for a few minutes,
    affect you emotionally?*

- *Is there a difference between the moving band experience when you focus on particular parts of the body and listening to your body as a whole?*

- *Does the meditation slow down your mind? Does it change the frequency or quality of your thoughts?*

— 2 —

watching now: the inner and outer shuttle

the present moment is a precious time. It is when feelings are felt, when decisions are made, when change is possible. But the power and magic of the present often eludes us. Instead, we may spend our time living in the past—with old hurts, old mistakes, with painful judgments about others and ourselves. Or we may be pulled into the future—with our worries and "what ifs" and visions of catastrophe. Meanwhile, the moments of our lives are lost.

Learning to live in the now takes a simple shift in your awareness. Instead of images from the past or the uncertain future, we observe the twin pillars of the moment: the experiences *inside* and *outside* our bodies. In the chapter on the Moving Band Meditation, you learned to observe what your body feels. Now you can practice the next step in awareness—shuttling back and forth between the inner and outer worlds.

Right now, close your eyes and notice the sensations in your body. What do you feel in your face and head? Your neck and shoulders? Notice the experience of breathing—the air going down the back of your throat, your ribs expanding, your diaphragm stretching. Observe any sensations in your chest and stomach. Now notice any feelings in your hips, buttocks, or genitals. Finally, pay attention to your legs and feet.

Now open your eyes and switch awareness to things outside your body. Notice what you see—the colors, shapes, and special qualities of the objects around you. Now observe the sounds in your environment—a ticking clock, traffic noise, the drone of distant voices. Now notice the feel of things—this book in your hands, the texture of the arm of your chair. Pay attention to any fragrances or other smells.

Close your eyes again. Shift focus to what your body feels. Scan from head to toe for each sensation. Some feelings may be uncomfortable or even painful. Some may be pleasant or pleasurable. It doesn't matter. Just watch what's happening inside, and stay with it for maybe two minutes.

Now open your eyes again, and shift back to the outside world. Notice what you see, hear, feel, and smell. Focus for two minutes on these experiences.

Shuttle back and forth between inner and outer experiences three or four more times. Try to notice something new as you make each switch. If thoughts show up or seem to interrupt the process, that's okay. Just notice them, and go back to focusing on the now.

When you are ready to stop shuttling back and forth, take a few minutes to think about these questions. Make sure not to look at the questions until you have had the experience of shuttling back and forth.

- *How is focusing on the now different from your normal consciousness?*

- *How does focusing on the now affect your mood?*

- *What qualities of the moment seem to pop out most?*

- *Are you more comfortable and relaxed focusing inside or outside your body?*

- *What qualities of the outside world seem most vivid and interesting to you?*

■ *What did you notice about your thoughts? Did your mind quiet down or get more active? Were there more or fewer worry thoughts? Were there more or fewer judgments?*

■ *How do you feel* now, *as opposed to just before this exercise?*

— 3 —

watching yesterday: memory versus observation

the past is a beautiful and disturbing place. It's where live our successes and losses; our moments of first discovery and cold disappointment. In the past we can take comfort or hide out. We can enjoy each moment of love and belonging or review a bitter rosary of failure.

The past is like a forest where you find majestic elk or see snakes hanging from the branches. And what shows up depends in part on what you're looking for. If you seek evidence you've been loved, chances are you'll find it. But if some dark part of you is bent on proving you're unworthy, you'll find reasons for that too.

So what do you do with this goldmine or minefield—your history? You can start to see it for what it is—a place your mind can go. Or leave. If it gives you refuge, enjoy it. If it hurts, come back to the present moment and calm yourself in the here and now.

The "now and then" shuttle is a way to facilitate the movement from past to present. This exercise allows you to migrate back and forth until time hopping feels easy. Start with a memory—any memory—that you can vividly recall. Anchor yourself there for a moment. See the shapes and colors of the scene. Listen to the sounds—wind or waves or voices. Feel that moment—the temperature, the textures.

Now shuttle to the present. What do you see right now? Let your eyes take in everything around you. Notice what you are hearing, even the tiniest of ambient sounds. What are your hands touching? How does the world press against your body? Do you feel warm or cold? Stay with the moment for a minute or two, and take it in.

Now return to the past—to another memory. It can be anything that comes to mind; it's completely arbitrary. Try to see it, hear it, and feel it. Give the memory a moment to come alive. Focus on the experience until you can feel what it was like to live it.

Switch again to the present. See your environment. Listen to whatever sounds there are. Notice what your skin tells you.

Now keep shuttling back and forth, returning to the past and present three more times, spending a few minutes in each place.

When you've completed the "now and then" shuttle, think about these questions:

- *Where do you tend to go in the past—to emotionally happy, neutral, or desolate places?*

- *Which feels calmer and more peaceful— the past or the present?*

- *Where do you feel better about yourself— present or past?*

- *Where would you like to spend more of your time—present or past?*

- *How difficult is it to shuttle to the present; is it hard to let go of the past?*

- *What would help you shift to the present, if you were stuck in memories you didn't like?*

— 4 —

pit bull thoughts

Pit bull thoughts are judgments, condemning evaluations of others or ourselves. There is a stock scene in countless movies where a dog grabs someone's pant leg and won't let go. The victim does a helpless little dance, trying to shake the animal, but the dog only holds on tighter. That's what pit bull thoughts do to you. They grab hold of your mind, keeping it in a tight grip of contempt, accusation, and blame.

This is not to say that judgment is always a problem. Some judgments are valuable and serve to protect us. Our minds sort things that we experience in our environment as good or bad—meaning they are likely to have a good or bad effect on us. This helps us decide quickly whether to approach or avoid something. But this vital process often runs amok, and our minds let the dogs out. One after another, they leap and tear at us—or at others we judge— doing great psychological damage.

Judgment thoughts, whomever they target, all hail from the same source: a belief in the way things should or shouldn't be. Many judgments grow from some ideal of beauty or attractiveness. Anything less than the ideal is labeled ugly. Some pit bull thoughts derive from rules about competence, hard work, or proper behavior. Anyone who breaks the rules seems worthy of blame.

You can change what happens with the pit bulls. The very first thing you can do is begin to notice them. Judgments have less power to hurt when you're paying attention. Do one or more of the following exercises to learn more about your pit bull thoughts:

- *When reading today's newspaper, make hatch marks on a note pad every time you experience a judgment.*

- *Visualize someone you don't like or don't approve of. It could be a political figure, a grumpy family member, or a competitor at work. Just keep your mind's eye focused on that person, and notice the judgments that arise.*

■ *Visualize a recent situation that upset you. Notice how the dogs attack the person who provoked you. Observe your judgments for a few minutes.*

■ *Visualize or stare in the mirror at a part of your body that you don't like. Listen to what you say to yourself.*

■ *Form a picture in your mind of something you did that you regret. Hold the image, and notice what your mind does. Observe the type (observation, memories, judgment, story telling, future thoughts) and the intensity of your judgments.*

Now it's time to reflect: what have you learned from this exercise about the ways you judge yourself and others?

■ *Do you tend to judge the behavior or the person as a whole?*

■ *What are the "shoulds" or rules of proper behavior that underlie some of your judgments?*

- *Woundings are your self-judgments—how do they impact your feelings about yourself?*

- *Do your judgments about others push you to action—to go on the attack or get revenge?*

- *Do your judgments about others push you to withdraw and protect yourself?*

Now comes the most important question. Since you can't turn your mind off, and judgments will always be there, do you want to change your *relationship* to judgment—to notice your judgments, yet take them less seriously? If you do, there are exercises later in this book that will help you.

seeing and feeling
versus judging

You see a gray Escalade—one of those Cadillac SUVs—and you think, "There's a gas guzzler that's helping to destroy the environment." While seeing and thinking are two different things, you may not notice that you've connected them together. The large gray car with a Cadillac insignia *becomes* the judgment "gas guzzler." So what you experience with your senses gets mixed up with what your mind tells you. Your judgments—which are assumptions and opinions, not reality—seem inseparable from the observable facts.

Learning to disentangle what you see, hear, and feel inside your body from how you judge what you see, hear, and feel is critical to understanding your mind and getting a healthy perspective on it. Here's what we're saying in a nutshell: *judgments aren't reality, but your mind thinks they are.*

The "seeing versus judging" shuttle is an exercise that can help to make this clear. Begin by noticing your breath. Now broaden your awareness to a sensation inside your body. Try to observe the sensation and just notice it. Now shift your focus to what you *think* about that feeling in your body. Does it feel good or bad? Do you like or dislike the sensation?

Now look around you. Find an object that's either black or brown. Study it for a moment and closely observe its shape and dimensions, its texture and any color variations. Now shift again to what you *think* about that object. Is the shape and color pleasing or displeasing? What do you think about its aesthetics? Does it look good or ugly? Is it new? Or old and damaged?

Now return to a feeling inside your body. Observe it first, then switch to evaluating your thought response. Now return back to the outer world and find an object of a different color. Notice all the details first, and then your judgment of what you notice. Keep the shuttle going for about ten minutes, or longer if you can.

When you've completed the "seeing versus judging" shuttle, take a few moments to think about these questions:

- *Do your judgments about an object feel clearly different from your observations? Or are they hard to separate?*

- *Were you starting to slip into judgments even before consciously making the switch?*

- *How easy or hard is it to stay in the observation-only mode?*

- *How easy or hard is it to let go of a judgment, once it forms, and shuttle to your next observation?*

— 6 —

storytelling thoughts

a favorite thing our minds like to do is tell stories. Not a story like your Uncle Charlie's endless saga about his travels in Kamchatka, but one that explains things, and answers the question "Why?" Our mental storytelling is really about getting at causes.

- *My father hasn't called because . . . he's angry with me.*

- *I don't have a boyfriend because . . . I'm unattractive and I irritate people.*

■ *My friends are late for my dinner party because . . . they didn't want to come.*

Our stories try to make sense of things that happen to us. They take ambiguous situations—things people do that are hard to read—and make up what seems a likely explanation.

In storytelling, we often mind-read, or make assumptions about what others think and feel about us. Our minds are story-making machines. They do it constantly. Compulsively. Thoughts that seek to explain the world are often helpful, and are a key part of our survival. But too often our stories are mere pieces of fiction.

This is when storytelling gets dangerous. We make things up, and then act as if they were absolute fact. Take the example used earlier: "My friends are late for my dinner party because they didn't want to come." Acting on this assumption, one might greet the tardy guests with coldness. Or decide to have nothing more to do with them. But what if that story was wrong? Our minds have a hard time telling the difference between fact and fiction, because we tend to believe what we think. Our stories, no matter how unlikely or absurd, always seem true to us. How, then, should we relate to our stories? We should see them as hypotheses, or as possibilities, as one in an endless string of ideas our minds have created. They are *not* absolute truth. They are mere thoughts.

Right now we'd like you to think about several stories that you return to again and again. These are stories about why certain things have happened or not happened to you; why you or others behave in certain ways.

Now ask yourself about each story: "Why did that happen?" or "Why is that true?" Whatever your answer, ask the question again. Keep asking until you run out of answers. After doing this exercise, you may notice several things. First, how easily your mind can cook up stories. More important, you may notice how shallow and not entirely believable some of those stories turn out to be.

Example: "My father hasn't called because he's angry at me." Why is that? "Because he thinks I'm lazy." Why is that? "Because I don't have a job." Why is that? "Because I keep sending out resumés and I get no calls." Why is that? "Because I have a stupid resumé." Why is that? "I don't know."

— 7 —

what's next: planning versus fortune telling

We carry our own crystal balls. A part of our mind is dedicated to predicting the future and avoiding potential harm. It's that little voice in your head that keeps whispering, "What if?" What if your daughter flunks out of school? What if that stomachache is an ulcer? What if sales fall and you lose the business? By trying to look ahead and by shining a light into the darkness of the future, we hope to stay safe. The problem is that we can get addicted to fortune telling, or to believing that by conceiving every possible danger, we will magically prevent it. So our life becomes a frightening string of worries that keeps us in a constant state of alarm.

Planning, while focused on the future, differs from fortune telling, because it doesn't create anxiety. It's about solving rather than anticipating problems. Planning usually gets down to specific steps for changing or coping with something. Whereas fortune telling is about figuring out the severity of a problem, planning is about cutting the problem down to size and finally overcoming it.

Take the example of Aaron Wolfson. The event of Hurricane Katrina and aftermath of a nearly abandoned city threatened to destroy his cooking school, The Savvy Gourmet. His first reaction was fortune telling, imagining the losses—house, business, and years of financial devastation. But he stopped worrying and started planning. He turned the cooking school into a supplier of fresh cooked food to thousands of rescue workers, police, and the media.

One of the best ways to deal with worry is to observe your mind and learn to distinguish planning from fortune-telling thoughts. Right now we'd like you to focus your attention on a recent worry. Give yourself a moment to really get into it. Notice how your mind starts to paint a dangerous future. Notice the way it seeks the most disturbing scenario. Now shift your focus to a single (possibly small) step you could take to reduce the risk or improve the situation. Don't try to figure out if it's practical or look for flaws in the plan. Just imagine this one problem-solving step.

Now find another recent worry. Focus on it till your mind begins fortune telling, then shift to finding that first, practical step you could take toward reducing the risk. When you've finished round two, repeat the process a third time.

At the end of the exercise, spend a few minutes considering the following questions:

- *Is there a difference in how you feel emotionally doing planning versus fortune telling?*

- *How difficult is it to shift from worrying to making a specific plan? How did it go by the third round?*

- *Did you find that worry kept creeping in as you attempted to plan? How did you refocus back to the process of planning?*

- *How could you become more alert to noticing your fortune-telling thoughts, and remember to shift to planning after you recognized some danger?*

— 8 —

future thoughts: fantasy versus observation

fantasies are a great vacation from real life. Romantic, sexual, success, or escape fantasies all have one thing in common: you leave the present moment to live somewhere else. You become a mental tourist.

Some fantasies are healthy. They create desire to make things happen in your life. Some help you visualize new goals. Some give you a needed moment of pleasure or stress relief.

But fantasies can harm. You can spend so much time in a pleasant but unlikely future that you lose contact with the present. Or fantasies can create such burning desires that everything else by contrast seems paltry and sad. Sometimes fantasies get in the way of making hard choices and real changes. You escape to the future instead of solving critical problems. We all pay for such escapes in the coin of depression and a sense that our lives have slipped out of control.

How do fantasies affect you? The best way to find out is to notice them, and see them in the context of the present moment. Right now, let yourself slip into a familiar daydream that is pleasant and reliable. Close your eyes and explore the image—notice the sights and sounds, and *feel* the experience. Savor the fantasy for a minute or two, trying to really *be* in the visualization.

Now open your eyes and shift your attention to the present moment. What do you see and hear? What sensations do you notice? Keep observing what your senses tell you for one to two minutes.

Now continue to shuttle back and forth between fantasy and the current moment. If the first fantasy you chose loses sharpness or appeal, find another. Keep shuttling for eight to ten minutes. Notice, as you transition back and forth, how it feels to move in each direction. Now take a few minutes to think about these questions:

- *How jarring or difficult is it to leave your fantasy and return to the present moment?*

- *Do you want to stay in the fantasy, or do you prefer the present moment?*

- *Is there anything in the present moment that makes it feel good to escape?*

- *How does fantasy impact your life, both positively and negatively?*

If fantasy is sometimes a problem for you, we suggest taking "reality breaks." Each time you find yourself drifting in a prolonged fantasy, take a deep breath and shift for one minute to the present. Notice what you see and hear, as well as what you feel inside your body. Ask this question: "What can I do right now to make my present moment better?"

the conveyor belt of experience

i t's time to put together everything you've experienced so far, and learn how to watch your mind. Knowing how to observe your thoughts is the first step to getting free from mental suffering.

Right now, place your attention on your breath. Notice the feeling of the cool air sliding down the back of your throat; observe the sensation of your chest expanding and your diaphragm stretching and releasing. As you exhale, notice how it feels throughout your body to let go.

Now, after a minute or two, shift your attention to what your mind is doing. Imagine that your thoughts are arriving via a conveyor belt of experience. It runs continuously right in front of you, carrying each thought as it forms in your mind. Your task is to sort the thoughts by putting one of four labels on each of them: (1) observation thought, (2) judgment, (3) future or "fortune-telling" thought, or (4) explaining or "storytelling" thought. For the purpose of this exercise, ignore memories, fantasies, and planning thoughts because that's too many to keep track of.

After getting centered and observing your breath, try to work at least three minutes on the conveyor belt. While observing your thoughts, imagine pasting sticky labels representing each type of thought on small boxes. Or you can just *say* the type of thought it is to yourself. If you miss a thought, don't worry about it. Just watch and label the next one.

When you've completed the conveyor belt of experience exercise, take a few minutes to think about these questions:

- *Of the four categories of thought you tracked, which one comes up most often?*

- *Which category of thought proved to be the most sticky and difficult to let go?*

- *Which category of thought triggered the strongest emotional reactions?*

- *Which category of thought was hardest to recognize and label? Did practice make it easier?*

- *To which category of thought would you like to be less attached, or take less seriously?*

PART II

~

what do your thoughts do to your life?

It's not that you have "wrong" thoughts, it's that you can spend too much time living *from* them, fused with them, rather than looking *at* them. We'd like for you to learn a very important skill—observing how your thoughts function. That is, what are the effects of your thoughts on your life?

Because you cannot choose which thoughts come to your mind, and because you cannot stop them from happening, it becomes imperative that you have some power over your *relationship* to a thought, and what you do as a result of that relationship. Believe it or not, this is more important than understanding, dissecting, or analyzing a thought's content, since often the "whys" are arbitrary and ever-changing.

You may ask, "Well then, how do I judge the effects of my thoughts?" We ask you to answer that question by studying how thoughts serve you. Do your thoughts help bring you closer to what you care deeply about in your life? Or do they function to keep you safe, but not actually nearer to what is important to you in life?

Consider the thought that comes into your head when the alarm clock goes off. "I don't want to go to work today." Is that thought "bad"? No, it's just that if you listened to that thought and took it literally, you'd stay in bed and miss work, risking your job and your means of supporting yourself. So, is this a thought that is not serving you well? It doesn't function in a helpful way in your life.

Here are some questions you might ask yourself in order to gauge the effects of a thought:

- *Is this thought serving me well or not?*

- *Is this thought helping me get closer to what matters most to me in life?*

- *If this thought were my chauffeur, would it be driving me in the direction I wanted to be heading?*

That is the litmus test of thoughts: How do they function in your life? Because thoughts are so automatic, you normally don't catch the difference between judging something about yourself versus just noticing with compassion and without judgment. Judgment is just another thought. You can use the exercises in this section to examine what your thoughts do to you and to your life. The more you are able to witness the thought process happening, the more flexibility you achieve and the more choice you have over the direction of your own life.

the workability test

the seven kinds of thoughts our minds make—memory, observation, planning, judging, fortune-telling, and storytelling—all help us function and thrive. All seven types of thoughts can be used in either helpful or harmful ways. Here are some examples:

- *Our **memory** helps us retrieve information. It can be a source of joy as we connect back to important moments and people in our lives. Some folks are consumed by memories of loss or failure. Others spend so much time in the past that they lose their footing in the present.*

- **Observing** *the moment can be calming. It also creates a rich and deeply felt experience of the now. But sometimes we need to stop observing and move into action, or else nothing will change.*

- **Judging** *helps you evaluate what's good or bad for you and stay away from harmful stuff. But it's also a club with which you can beat yourself and others. Harsh judgments can damage both your self-esteem and every close relationship.*

- **Storytelling** *is essential for explaining and making sense of things. But as we discussed earlier, it often runs amok with mind reading and the most negative interpretation of events.*

- **Planning (future thoughts)** *helps us solve problems and prepare for the future. But some people spend so much time planning and preparing that their current lives become a misery. Some years ago, the* National Enquirer *carried a story about a man who built his own RV. When he finished ten years, one heart attack,*

*and no vacations later, his neglected wife
and kids wondered what the point was.*

■ **Fortune telling (future thoughts)** *helps
you predict the future and avoid life's
potholes. If you know a lion lives in a
certain cave, fortune telling helps you
anticipate being eaten if you venture
there. But fortune telling can turn into a
torture, in which you sink into "what if"
and imagine an endless string of possible
but unlikely catastrophes.*

■ **Fantasies (future thoughts)** *can be
a source of pleasure as you imagine
vacations, longed-for events, and future
achievements. But fantasies can be
dangerous because they often prevent
you from taking the practical steps to
make them come true. Or they end up
depressing you because the fantasy makes
your current life seem drab and empty by
comparison.*

Here's the million-dollar question: How do you know
when your mind's gone off the rails? How do you know
when you're buying into thoughts that don't make sense?
Remember—your mind tends to believe everything it

thinks. The answer lies in something called *workability*. How well is a certain, oft-repeated thought working for you? Is it helping you or not?

Let's use storytelling thoughts as an example. Can you remember several stories you tend to use a lot? These are stories about why certain things happen or don't happen, or about why you or others behave in specific ways. Now ask yourself these questions about each story: How has it worked for you? Does the story motivate you or make you give up? Does it make you feel good or bad about yourself? Does it help you do the things that matter to you, or does it make you afraid to move?

In general, a thought is workable when it enhances, expands, or opens your life; when it solves rather than creates problems. Thoughts are *not* workable when they constrict, inhibit, or close off your life.

Right now, we'd like you to explore this workability criterion with some of your frequent thoughts. Examine carefully the *effects* of each thought. Does it help you live more fully, or is it shutting you down? If a thought isn't working for you, it's time to stop believing in it. Instead, just notice it so you can begin to take it less seriously.

mental marriages

We have thoughts that automatically occur, and we don't really have the ability to suppress or stop them from happening. For instance, without trying to, fill in the blank words:

Rome wasn't built in a _____.

Rudolph the Red-Nosed _____.

Read one more, and try not to think of the word that follows:

Step on the crack; break your mama's _____.

Here's the rub: this automatic linking occurs with your own thoughts and feelings. You have your own personalized built-in creative sayings like these clichés. Sometimes they come from your own experience, and at other times you've picked them up from god knows where. So, instead of Rome wasn't built in a day, yours might be something like, "If I have to speak in public tomorrow, I will panic. I should stay at home." Perhaps your mind is telling you this because you've panicked in a public speaking situation before. Staying at home on subsequent occasions has made you feel safe. So you've learned the association *public speaking-panic-home,* and your mind can dish it up for you in a split second. Now, what if the speech is important to you, and you care about expressing all of the information you've spent time preparing? Would buying into that thought, "I will panic; stay at home" serve you well? Will it help you lead a full, engaging life, or will listening to the thought keep you from doing what matters to you?

It's important to notice how your mind works and how it's creating scenarios and solutions that are just automatic responses. Your life becomes more and more narrow when you avoid doing things because your thoughts predict the outcome.

Now that you know you cannot stop your mind from making associations and giving you advice, with practice, you can work on accepting those thoughts and not allow them to direct your actions.

judging everything

most of us do a good bit of judging. We can find flaws in virtually anything:

- *That tree over there—it's a bit lopsided.*

- *The chair I'm sitting in—a little too soft and spongy.*

- *The sunset—not enough flaming orange.*

- *This park—the lawns are a little brown.*

- *My mother-in-law—too critical.*

Right now do this exercise. Look around your environment. Whether you are in a room or somewhere outside, let your eyes roam and settle on various objects. Now see if you can make a judgment about what you're looking at. Notice any flaw it might have. Keep going—moving your attention from thing to thing—and evaluating each one in turn.

Here's the question: Is there anything that *can't* be evaluated, that doesn't have some flaw? Answer: Probably not. This simple fact becomes important because every one of us experiences moments when we actively look for flaws—in ourselves, in others, in the objects around us. And we can always find them.

Why do we judge? What drives us at times to seek the negative? Listed below are some reasons why we make judgments. Give a little thought to each one, and see which might apply to you.

- *To predict or solve a problem (the most helpful kind of judgment).*

- *To protect us from disappointment.*

- *To try to fix or perfect ourselves or others.*

- *To prove ourselves better than someone else (they have flaws we don't possess).*

- *To prove that we're as bad as we think, or as bad as someone else (usually our parents) thought.*

- *To punish ourselves for mistakes or wrongdoing.*

- *To get relief from hurt or shame (by judging those who hurt or shamed us).*

Sometimes knowing the function of a thought gives us perspective. And helps us take our thoughts a little less seriously.

— 13 —

what's this thought trying to do?

every thought has a function. And thoughts that show up over and over can only do so because they provide you something important. Oft-repeated thoughts are highly rewarding. They may protect you from pain, remind you of your core identity, keep you from doing scary things, or dozens of other functions. Even painful thoughts are rewarding. Their job, invariably, is to protect you from an emotion or experience that's even worse. Whatever the purpose of a thought, you can bet that it has arrived in your mind *at this exact moment* for a reason.

Knowing why a thought shows up can give you some distance and perspective. Our thoughts often resemble political speeches. They sound true and convincing until we learn Senator So and So supports a new highway because a resort he owns would make millions when the highway is built. Before you buy a thought, and start acting as if it's true, we encourage you to look deeper and seek its real purpose. Here are some examples. You might have a thought whose function is:

- *To remember that you are your mother's (father's) daughter or son (meaning you're like them).*

- *To scare you.*

- *To keep you following the rules (handed down by family, or learned during painful experiences).*

- *To punish you for your sins and mistakes.*

- *To try to fix or perfect you.*

- *To paralyze you.*

- *To show you all your flaws.*

- *To keep the approval of _____ (fill in the blank).*

- *To keep you confused so you do nothing.*

- *To keep you from ever taking a risk.*

- *To make sure you never feel pain.*

- *To prove you are blameless.*

- *To prove you are helpless (or a victim).*

- *To get you to give up.*

Your mind has a million reasons. Those above are a tiny sample of the universe of motives for a thought. As an exercise, we'd like you to examine three recent thoughts that touched you emotionally. Select:

- *A thought that scared you.*

- *A thought that made you feel bad about yourself (unworthy, ashamed, guilty).*

- *A thought that irritated you.*

Now ask yourself for each: What's that thought trying to do? What urge does it create? And if you gave into that urge, if you acted on it, what effect would that have on:

- *Your worth*

- *Your identity*

- *Your goals*

- *Your fears*

- *Your relationships (past or present)*

- *Your shoulds (the rules you were given to live by)*

Next time a thought comes up—and you've learned its function—thank your mind for what it was trying to do.

- *Thank you, mind, for trying to . . . keep me from achieving anything.*

- *Thank you, mind, for helping me . . . be what my dad always said I'd be.*

- *Thank you, mind, for keeping me . . . a victim.*

- *Thank you, mind, for trying to make me . . . perfect.*

— 14 —

what world are your thoughts making?

We create the world we live in with our thoughts. Here's how:

- *What we think, we believe.*

- *What we believe becomes our reality.*

- *Whatever is our reality becomes the basis of our hopes, fears, and choices.*

- *What we choose becomes our life.*

Though our thoughts are nothing more than the ephemeral firing of neurons, we take them so seriously that they can frighten us, make us hate ourselves, or make us despise someone else. Our thoughts have the power to paralyze us, or start wars.

In truth, we are all painters that let our minds apply the colors, textures, and shapes to the canvas of our lives. And we are programmers who weave our thoughts into a little universe with its own rules and systems and outcomes.

If your thoughts are making your world, it might be helpful to take a good look at the world you're fashioning. In this exercise, we'd like you to focus on thoughts about who you are and what you expect in life—from others, from fate. Next, look beyond these thoughts to the world they create. Is it bleak, with dangerous and difficult figures competing for scarce resources? Is it warm and sunny, with generous and caring people looking after each other? Is it a place where no one is safe, or a place with people you can trust? Is it a world of struggle and failure, where you can't buy a break, or one where hard work succeeds in the end?

Now write a description of the world your thoughts make. What do the people do there? How do they survive? What are the rules? What are the dangers? How do you fit in this place? When finished, ask yourself if this is where you want to live. Remember, this world is no more real or substantial than a string of words. If you don't want to live here, it's time to stop believing everything you think.

— 15 —

the great escape

Certain thoughts function to help give you instant relief. You feel pain of some kind, and there's a built-in mechanism—designed especially just for you by you—to offer escape from negative feelings. You probably designed your relief after certain experiences in your past that felt uncomfortable. You figured out ways to avoid the pain, to cover it up, or to flee as quickly as possible.

Your body is hardwired to do this because of the fight or flight response to danger. Since the beginning of the human species, when faced with life-threatening situations, such as a confrontation with a tiger, the body would physiologically change in order to literally fight or flee. The amazing thing about your brain is that all you have to do is think about a threat in order for your body to respond with fight or flight. It doesn't take a tiger to respond like this; all you need to do is think of something from your own unique experiences that frightens you.

In your haste to flee, you may have developed ways to escape from pain that do not to serve you well in life. For instance, many people eat, drink, work, etc. as ways to avoid the scary emotions. Great escape thoughts are thoughts you have that urge you to do something to not feel hurt, or sadness, or anger. Unfortunately, the escape instinct turns out to keep you from accepting the initial pain that you must feel in order to heal.

What are some great escape thoughts you might have when faced with pain of some kind? On a separate piece of paper, write down at least three escape thoughts. Then answer these questions:

- *Do you fantasize and neglect your work?*

- *Do you shop, or run, or clean your house with a toothbrush?*

- *Are these behaviors working for you?*

- *Are you willing to feel the initial feelings and work with those feelings first?*

By avoiding your feelings, you have two layers of pain instead of the one. Those escape thoughts that urge you to avoid feeling something are just thoughts. You do have the power to catch a thought happening, and you can choose to respond to the thought in a new way. When you know the thought is an escape thought, you can consider whether it is leading you in a direction you want to head.

■ *Is it aligned with your values, or what matters to you?*

■ *Are you able to have the escape thought while sitting with your initial feeling and using mindful observation to let the thought happen without acting on it?*

the seducer

You think because your mind is a part of you, that must mean it's on "your side." But sometimes, thoughts are not on your side, they actually serve to detract you. Did you ever have a "so-called" friend in high school? Someone who acted like your friend, but who actually got you in trouble, or seduced you into doing poorly in a certain class? Or maybe your friend lured you into smoking or drinking. Picture this kid. He smokes, he's got the badass leather jacket, he doesn't wash his hair, and his eyes are shifty. Some of our thoughts are like this kid. While they look like they might serve us, in reality, they are destructive. Seducer thoughts usually sound like:

"I don't really have to get that memo done today."

"Well, maybe this once I'll skip the mandatory meeting."

"She doesn't really need my help."

"I'm sure I can make up the work next week."

These thoughts are just the bad kid in high school cajoling you to do things against your better judgment. These thoughts are attacking your well-being. They do not function as positive behavioral directors in your life. The bad kid thought is not leading you in the direction of your values! In the moment, this thought can serve as instant relief (from responsibility, or facing something you're scared to face), but truly, in the long run they are not in your best interest. Think about what matters to you more: getting rid of a task, or taking care of tasks that help you get ahead in life?

■ *Take a moment to reflect on at least one important task that you know you'd feel better accomplishing rather than putting off or procrastinating.*

■ *Let that seducer come to mind. Accept the voice of distraction as a voice, an angle, but not a reality.*

- *Now let the seducer fade into the background, and bring to mind the task that you might be avoiding.*

- *Take in a deep breath to the count of three. Exhale on the count of three. Now visualize yourself taking care of the task.*

- *Each time the seducer tries to lure you away from your goal, let it fade into the background as you bring to mind the task that you want to accomplish.*

Once the task is complete, you'll feel like the class president instead of the smoker in the back of the building.

— 17 —

rogue thoughts

ost people have experienced an occasional bizarre thought totally unrelated to what is happening in the moment. You might be talking to your boss, and then unexpectedly picture her head exploding. Or, out of nowhere, you might picture poking your friend in her eye in the middle of a nice conversation over a cup of tea. You're sitting quietly at a dinner party, and then have the thought that you're going to say something incredibly shameful, embarrassing yourself and your innocent spouse.

In fact, 90 percent of people have rogue thoughts—blasphemous, sexually inappropriate, harming, etc. These thoughts might be dark, violent or destructive, and you're not even aware of having this kind of intent. You might wonder, "What kind of person am I to have a thought like that?" Remember, a thought is just a thought. Notice that you haven't actually ever acted on one of these rogue thoughts. They come to your mind for an instant or two and then pass. Rogue thoughts never lead to action. That's because there's a difference between a thought and an impulse. An impulse usually has a motivation behind it—you want that drink, or you want to buy those shoes. Whereas a thought, especially a rogue thought, does not have motivation behind it. You don't really want to poke your friend in the eye or make a spectacle of yourself at a party.

Remember a rogue thought you've had in the past. Now hold that thought in your mind. Notice that it has no power to do anything. It's just a thought, not a reality. Thank your mind for that weird thought, and see if you might even enjoy how amazing and unusual it is.

— 18 —

the thought storm

the rule of the brainstorm is that no idea is stupid. Everyone has the right to offer their opinion and to throw out a suggestion that might help the group achieve their goal. The key is to first identify the goal of the group. Otherwise, how can you tell which opinion serves the group best? If there's no goal, then the discussion is one without a point in mind. No brainstorm thoughts are realized during the brainstorm; they are merely heard. Everyone offers an idea of what you might do, what you could do, and how you might do it. Some listen and just ponder what the others say. Each person has their own function as part of the group. One may be the conservative who warns against risky ventures. Another may be inspired and passionate and lead the group in new directions, perhaps without caution.

Imagine your mind functions like a brainstorming session. There are a bunch of well-meaning ideas being tossed around. Some are meant to protect you from pain, some to help you get a task done, and others want growth and progress. Imagine that you could hear the ideas in your mind as if each one was the voice of reason at a brainstorming session. Since none are yet literal truths and still in the idea phase, step back and just listen objectively to each opinion before buying into a specific thought as *the way* to get where you want to be.

Let's say you're single, invited to a party, and have a hard time meeting people. Suddenly, the brainstorm is in session. Each member has a different idea.

"I don't know how to get there anyway."

"Well, I could Mapquest it or get a ride with a friend."

"No one's going to talk to me, why bother?"

"I look too unattractive right now."

"But I want to meet people! I haven't socialized in over three months!"

How would you choose which idea to listen to? They're all reasonable, after all. Some will give you instant relief from your anxiety about going. Others help you get closer to what you want, which is to meet someone.

Now, think of something you have been wanting and also debating mentally.

Ask yourself:

- *What do I really want?*

- *Is this going to help me get closer to what is important to me?*

- *Are there thoughts that mean well and also serve to keep me from moving forward?*

- *Can I listen to the different ideas as if they are all well-intentioned and still choose what's best for me at this time in my life?*

bossy thoughts

You don't want to let your thoughts boss you around, because sometimes thoughts are being just that— bossy. They tell you what to do, like a big bully in the schoolyard.

Thoughts driven by anxiety can feel bossy. Anxiety wants to get its way. If you are about to go out with a new group of friends with whom you're not entirely comfortable, your bossy thoughts might try and stop you from hanging out. They start poking and prodding you to stay home, disengage, and just watch TV where it's nice and safe on the couch. The anxiety comes on strong, just like that schoolyard bully. At first you may cower. But you have a choice.

You can think about those thoughts as if they are just being bossy and not as something that has to direct your actual behavior.

If a bossy thought is standing in the way of something you want to do, or something you know would be good for you, take the following steps:

- *When those bossy thoughts start coming on, first stop and recognize, "These are bossy thoughts!"*

- *Next, consider other reasons that you want your experience, even with those bossy thoughts chattering away in your mind.*

- *Notice the thought, but* choose *your actions. Do you truly want to change your behavior because of a thought?*

- *Is buying into this thought more important, or saying, "Oh, I'm going to have this thought and do something different anyway," or "I'm going to, because I* choose *to experience this situation, and see where it might lead"?*

stale bread

Sometimes we hang onto thoughts that are as stale and hard as last week's baguette. For instance, maybe you've been having the same thought for years ("I can't do new things," or "Why would anyone at the party like me?").

Take stock of the stale bread thoughts inventory in the cupboard of your mind. In your journal, write down at least five thoughts that you've harbored for years. Use thoughts that you know don't serve you. If you think of one that haunts you now, work with that one. Let's say you got hurt in a past relationship, and the thought that stuck with you is, "Men/women aren't safe." It's a thought that made sense at that time in the *past*. You got hurt, and you want to prevent it from happening again. But is that thought going to keep you from pain? Will adhering to that thought keep from opening your eyes to what it's like to experience closeness with someone now? Make a commitment to catch that thought as it occurs now, and note, "There's my stale bread thought. It's keeping me in the prison of my past. It's not a reflection of what is happening here, today."

— 21 —

you are not a thought

a thought is just words. Our minds tend to take words literally, and before we know it, the words of a thought become truth in our mind. If we can begin to notice that a thought is just words, we will take our thoughts less seriously.

Let's start with the word "spider." When you think "spider," what does it look like in your mind? Can you see it crawling? You may even feel a little anxious if spiders scare you in real life. You don't even have to see the spider in order for it to scare you, because just thinking something can make you feel as if you are experiencing the "real thing."

Imagine yourself going to work naked. Picture yourself walking through the front door of the office with no clothes on, and imagine the expressions on the faces of your coworkers. Does this image make you blush or cringe, as if you had really just gone to work naked? The mind is a powerful manufacturer of reality! But reality is not always what you think.

Right now, bring to mind a negative word that you think about yourself, like "unattractive," or "boring." Does it feel like a word, or does it feel true? This may sound crazy, but go and find a sticky label that you can attach to the front of your shirt. It will need to work as a nametag. Think of one negative word that describes something you don't like about yourself. Maybe sometimes you feel like a "big mouth," a "fake," "stupid," "fearful," or "anxious." Whatever the word is, write it down on your label and stick it to your jacket or shirt. Today, it's your nametag.

Notice that it's a word. These awful feelings you have about yourself are just a word, a name, a label you've given yourself. It's not the truth, or the only real thing about you. If someone in your family sees it and asks, "What the hell is that?" hopefully you can begin to even laugh at the one silly word.

just because you think it, doesn't make it so

Close your eyes and sit in silence for one minute. What goes through your mind? Did you worry about what you have to do at work tomorrow? Did you wonder if your kids were doing their homework? When you opened your eyes, had anything different actually happened in that minute? Mostly likely, nothing happened. You're still sitting in the same room, and your worries and ideas have not yet changed anything. You haven't done any of those tasks you need to do for work. You haven't asked your child to do her/ his homework. What if a good friend called you, and you ended up talking for an hour? You'd forget you'd even had those thoughts. They'd vanish into the past.

When you realize how transitory thoughts can be, perhaps even difficult ones can lose some of their hold over you. They aren't any stronger than others, they're not made of different chemicals in your mind, and even if they were, it wouldn't matter. You can still learn that even when you have a thought, you can behave differently from the thought. If you said to yourself right now, "I'm a genius," would you suddenly be a genius?

Now think of three things to tell yourself that you don't like about yourself, like:

"I'm lazy."

"I'm fat."

"I don't know how to change."

Does having the thought, "I'm lazy," make you instantly lazy? Or can you still get up when the alarm goes off, have coffee, and go to work for eight hours?

You can think, "I'm fat," even though your doctor told you at your last physical that you're in great shape.

You can hop up and down on the couch and think, "I'm sitting on the couch."

You can think, "I'm so boring!" and still plan a fun date with your husband by calling the theater, buying tickets, and getting a babysitter for the night.

Try these exercises:

- *Make a list of typical thoughts like these that you have. These are self-deprecating thoughts you tell yourself about a love relationship, a friendship, or about yourself.*

- *Make a point of having one of those thoughts, and then deliberately do something that goes beyond that thought. Do something that is the opposite of that thought.*

- *When you've done that, look back over your list, and try out a few more over the next week. This puts distance between you and that thought, and maybe the thought will even start to dissolve.*

— 23 —

rainy day acceptance

most of us have had the experience of having a great day all planned out, only to wake up to the sound of rain. At first, we struggle with it, even argue with it, thinking maybe it'll clear up. It wasn't supposed to rain after all. Soon we realize, well, it's raining, and no amount of frustration is going to stop the water from falling from the sky. So, we have to change our plans. We cancel the picnic, or the drive out to the beach, and we decide to do something different—something that matters to us, but that isn't what we'd originally intended.

You might have thoughts that are like rain from time to time—thoughts that you really don't want to be having.

You don't want to think something negative about your new job, or be pessimistic about a date. But try as you may, the rainy thoughts keep pouring in and soaking your attitude.

You can choose to do something different than what your rainy thoughts have planned for you. Instead of caving in to the negativity or dismal outlook, rearrange your plans. Take action towards something you know you want to experience even with the rain of thoughts. This is the fabulous choice that you have—to change a course of action and go for it anyway. Perhaps you're pessimistic about a work meeting. While you recap all of the miserable meetings you've been to, follow through on this one, and carry your rainy thoughts along as you get dressed, answer the door, and step into the world.

the one-track mind

Occasionally it can feel like no matter how hard you try, you cannot get a particular thought out of your mind. It might be a worry thought that your mind plays over and over by waking you up in the middle of the night, or distracting you at work. Perhaps you exchanged angry words with a friend or family member that left you full of unresolved emotions. It might also be a fear thought, like a phobic response to something you know you have to do, such as speaking in public, taking an airplane, or going to a social event.

The thought might even feel obsessive, as it became the dominant mode, overshadowing whatever else may have actually been happening. It's hard to notice what other experiences may be occurring when you have a one-track mind, but that doesn't have to be true.

You have a choice and a skill you can learn. The choice is to learn to pay attention to other sensations, feelings, and even other thoughts when your mind feels stuck on something fearful, negative, judgmental, or distracting. The skill is mindfulness. Mindfulness can help you become aware of the thought that is bothering you, as well as other experiences that are true. For instance, if you are having a fear thought, you can take a moment to notice what else is going on for you. You might look up at the sky, and notice the clouds, or the light or the darkness of a night sky. It's like taking off thought blinders, and looking around at what else there is. You can open your mind and your awareness.

If you currently have a thought that is plaguing you, bring that thought to mind for the mindfulness exercise below. If you don't have a thought that's bothering you right now, just practice the mindfulness exercise with a previous preoccupation. Or simply practice mindfulness so that when you do have that one-track-mind experience, you will more readily remember that you have a skill to use. Read the exercise several times, so that you can then close your eyes and move through it on your own. Spend anywhere from five minutes to an hour, or whatever feels comfortable to practice experiencing what is happening here and now.

- *Sit comfortably on a chair or lie on your bed.*

- *Take three deep breaths in this position.*

- *Simply notice if the dominant thought or any other thought comes to mind. Don't judge the thought as right or wrong.*

- *Notice while having this thought, that other experiences are also happening as your body rests in this position. Feel the way your body is contacting the chair or bed. Does the bedding feel soft under your weight? How does the seat of the chair feel beneath your bottom? How does the back of the chair feel supporting your back?*

- *Scan your body from head to toe, spending at least five breaths on a different body part as you move your way down toward your feet. Begin with your head. Can you feel any tension in your face, brow, or jaw? Take three breaths here. Now feel your neck and shoulders. Are the muscles starting to relax with each breath? If they aren't, just notice and move on to your chest and abdomen. Are your chest and stomach rising with each breath? Now keep moving down your body, noticing each part, and observing any aches or pains or pleasurable sensations. Keep moving on with awareness of another body part until you've reached your toes.*

■ *Now, notice any emotions you are feeling. Is there more than one? For instance, you may feel both scared and excited. Notice that as you feel one emotion, it may change as you focus upon it. Notice the other thoughts that surface in addition to the dominant one. Pay attention to the other thoughts for a moment, then shift back to the dominant one and notice if it has changed at all.*

By the end of the exercise, you will have become aware of other sensations, thoughts, or feelings that you have in addition to the one-track thought.

— 25 —

bringing a thought into your awareness

let's say you have a thought that you are avoiding, a thought you are scared to have because it might bring up certain emotions. We have intense as well as mundane kinds of thoughts that we avoid. For instance, have you ever had a little pain in your tooth, but just didn't want to call the dentist? You kind of knew you needed to think about it, but you just kept putting it on the back burner. You avoided it. Avoiding a thought does not make a thought disappear. Those more important to your well-being can fester until they become an underlying anxiety or sadness in your life.

As you release all of the energy it takes to keep them at bay, the simple act of bringing these thoughts into your awareness can send a sigh of relief through your whole being.

Now, find a quiet place where you can sit comfortably for at least five minutes and try this exercise:

- *Spend a moment searching your mind for a thought you've been struggling to avoid and bring it into your awareness.*

- *Just notice if other thoughts immediately occur, as distractions or because they are connected to the first thought.*

- *Allow those other thoughts to just happen, and then let them move on.*

- *Bring the original thought back into focus.*

- *Take a few deep breaths with the thought in your mind.*

- *Observe the thought without trying to change it, argue with it, or minimize it.*

- *Let it be what it is—a thought.*

- *Imagine it almost as a friend, or someone you would just listen to without judgment.*

- *Notice that your mind is having the thought, and at the same time you are able to witness the thought as just a thought.*

- *Notice that you are not your thoughts, that you are the observer self that is watching a thought.*

- *Notice that the thought in and of itself is not harmful or unfriendly.*

- *Now take a good five minutes to breathe, and let that thought be. Give it some airtime. Maybe all it needs is to be set free.*

looking for flaws

You'd think that after having been with you all your life, your mind would be your friend, your trustworthy companion, and here to look out for your interests. The truth is your mind is doing its job according to what it's been taught so far. Your mind experienced your history and it shares your memories. It's possible that your mind developed a safety plan to keep you from harm, which worked at some point early on. For example, suppose your parents criticized you in an effort to make you perform "better" in life. They believed that by pointing out flaws, they could help you become perfect, or near perfect. They believed that pointing out your flaws served you well—that it was the only way to help you grow and compete in this dog-eat-dog world. You accepted that because that is how you got approval, and maybe even love.

Your mind listened and responded by taking on that role for you. Now, when you achieve something, or receive praise, your mind automatically jumps at this opportunity to make you "better" by pointing you in the direction of perfection. Your mind has become so narrow that it can only hear and search for imperfections. It's lost sight of the goal, and what was that again? Oh, to be perfect.

Do you want simply to do well in life, to be loved, and to feel connected to others? Do you want to have compassion for your imperfections, and to be able to see them as opportunities for growth? If these don't resonate, take a moment to consider your own values. What is important? Would you like to feel love and acceptance for yourself? Would it feel good to be able to accept that sometimes you do things well, and are deserving of praise?

Do you remember the last time your boss, a good friend, or your spouse expressed how well you're doing? What happens when you hear those positive words? Does your mind quickly think of reasons that they may not be true, or how another negative quality overshadows the positive one? To what is that inner critical voice in service? Is it helping you? If you compare yourself to some unrealistic ideal, you may just die before you've reached it.

Consider that this tendency to spotlight failures and flaws is keeping you from what is important to you and what you might crave: love, compassion, and self-acceptance. Take a moment to consider how it would feel to have someone give you positive feedback. In this moment, hear the positive words in your mind. When your mind starts feeding you the negative counterthoughts, just notice them happening and let them be. They're just chatter—more pit bull stuff. For what is that really of service? Is it in the service of your interests, or of what is important to you? Now hear those positive words again in your mind, and let them in.

— 27 —

thoughts like stars

a continuous part of you has existed for your entire life. This deeper part of yourself has been present and enduring throughout all of the pain, the joy, the growth, and the struggles you've experienced. It's called your "observer self." In everyday life, you tend to live *from* your thoughts, as if you *are* your thoughts. However, a subtle but powerful shift occurs when you realize you can learn to witness thoughts as if they were stars in the galaxy. It is your observing self that is the galaxy holding the stars.

Take a few minutes to sit somewhere comfortable and take a few deep breaths. If your chest is rising and falling, focus on getting the breath to go deeper in your abdomen, so that your stomach rises and falls with each breath. Next, remember something that happened to you on your last birthday. Can you see what you were wearing? Were you with friends or were you alone? Were you celebrating, or working late that night? As you remember that day, can you notice that you—the person who is sitting here now—were there, experiencing that day? Just as you are able to sit here now and recall that day, your observing self is able to experience the present moment. That is, just as you can remember who you were last year, you can also observe who you are now. All that you feel, think, and do is observable when you step back into the seat of the witness. The observer self looks at the thoughts your beautiful mind produces and sees them for what they are—just memories, images, and ideas. Nothing more; nothing less.

— 28 —

chain gang

Thoughts run in packs. Rather than show up as individual ideas, they're often part of a group. Here's how it works. Let's say you made a mistake. Suddenly every experience in your whole life that resembles that mistake automatically gets linked to it. Your mind makes the association and trots out memories of these previous errors, one after another. One screw-up becomes the first link in a long chain of similar memories.

Our mind sorts every experience by categories. If you have a big box of experiences labeled "got rejected," then every new rejection tends to trigger memories of the others.

For each new rejection, you go through the whole box, scene by scene, until you're thoroughly depressed.

Because each life experience is linked to many others that have the same theme or emotional tone, we often find ourselves stuck on a chain gang. We get hit with one painful memory after another. And no amount of regret or struggle to escape sets us free.

Getting off the chain gang requires two things. The first is to observe the chaining process, to really see each link that holds us to our pain. The second is to turn our attention to the here and now. Mindfulness breaks obsessive chains by focusing on the simple human experiences that make up our lives.

So let's make our escape. Right now, focus on one of the following:

- *A worry that seems to lead to a whole sequence of catastrophic events.*

- *A failure that somehow feels connected to other mistakes from the past.*

- *A loss that feels a part of a matrix of similar losses.*

- *A judgment or offensive comment that reminds you of similar experiences (either with the same person or others).*

Now observe the chain of thoughts. Notice how one leads to another. See how each thought or memory has a "piling on" effect that intensifies your distress. Just keep watching one thought slip into the next; observe your subjective sense of heaviness, as the chain grows longer.

Now shift your attention to your breath. Let the chain go as you feel the air slip down your throat and into your lungs. Feel your diaphragm stretch, feel the release as you begin to exhale. Notice that the chain gang thoughts may be pushing to get in. Notice that your mind may even *want* to embrace these thoughts.

Keep attending to your breath. Even as chain gang thoughts pull you away, bring your attention back to your breathing. Stay with the *feeling* in your throat, lungs, and diaphragm. As new thoughts appear, notice them and return to your breath. Your body and your breathing are a safe harbor in that old chain gang life.

move your feet

Often, a thought starts in your head and travels to your feet. You think something, and then before you know it, you end up doing it. This can be an automatic phenomenon. It's important to notice that you have the ultimate power of choice. What will your feet do when your head has a thought?

First, spend an hour, or even the day, noticing when a thought leads to an action, or when it does not. Start by noticing the simple innocuous thoughts like, "I'm thirsty," which leads to you to getting up, going to the sink, and getting a glass of water. The thought traveled from your head to your feet, which then carried you to the sink. Or, you have the thought, "I don't want to go to school today." But you get up and go to school anyway.

Then, there are thoughts that can become like road-blocks. Just notice these too. "I need to exercise, *but* I could just go visit my friend on the way home tonight and maybe have a drink." Notice that these thoughts often have the word "but" in them. What actions follow that kind of thought? What do you actually do after having such a thought? In this case, you end up shifting back to your value and asking your friend to go for a walk instead of having a drink.

Consider fear thoughts. Begin to notice that when you feel nervous about something, you might have a thought or urge that helps you ease the fear. For instance, you have the thought, "I'm nervous about my boyfriend's mother coming to dinner." Next thing you know, you have the urge to do some online shopping, which might ease the tension. You can have this impulse and do something different. Rather than distracting yourself, you can instead choose to start reading through cookbooks to help prepare for your visit.

In a journal, or on a piece of paper, write down at least ten different thoughts you have that lead to actions. Start to recognize that thoughts travel from your head to your toes, if you let them. Now ask yourself this important question: Must this be so? Do thoughts automatically have to travel from head to toes? The goal is to become aware of choice. You have choice over where your feet go, and which thoughts you want directing your actions.

PART III

~

stop believing
everything
you think

for your whole life, your mind has been chattering away. And you've been listening to it as if your mind were the Oracle at Delphi, as if it spoke only truth. Your mind has called you hurtful names, told you what people think of you, and shown you terrifying pictures of what is to come.

You know now that your mind can't help it. No matter what, your mind is going to keep thinking. You can't make your mind better behaved; you can only change your *relationship* to it. Instead of taking every thought as gospel, you can choose to stop believing everything you think. This section of the book will teach you to watch your mind from a distance, to observe—without believing or rejecting—a stream of thoughts.

Why not work on changing your negative or unproductive thoughts to more positive ones? Because, when you try to change a thought, you're still in the trenches doing battle with your thought. When you simply observe your thoughts, you're declaring a truce. You and your thoughts can peacefully coexist.

No matter how certain your mind seems to be, a thought is just a thought. It isn't reality, and it isn't your enemy. The exercises you're about to experience are going to help you enjoy your mind while taking it much less seriously.

— 30 —

labeling thoughts

having a thought and being a thought are not the same. It's like the difference between *having* a pile of dishes in the sink and *being* a mess. Or having made a mistake versus being a failure. Thoughts are temporary and ephemeral. They occur during a moment in time, and often get erased a second later.

This is important: Thoughts are not real; they're not a thing. They're literally nothing. They are phantasms; they are bridges, living just long enough to get us to the next thought. We will have millions of thoughts in our lifetime, most of which we'll immediately forget, and none of which define who we really are.

When the Buddha was a young man, he learned something that would be a wellspring for everything he later taught. Gautama Siddhartha discovered that thoughts are the source of suffering when we believe them, when we take them seriously, and when we mistake them for what is real and true. Only when we recognize the delusion that thoughts and reality are the same thing, only when we begin to *detach* and gain distance from our thoughts, can true peace be found.

One way to stop *being* your thoughts is to simply label them for what they are.

"I'm having the thought that John is mad at me."

"I'm having the thought that a storm is coming."

"I'm having a thought that I need to change careers."

"I'm having a thought that I'm not attractive."

When you label your thoughts in this way, it's easier to realize that they aren't necessarily true. Each thought is merely a link in the long chain of your conscious life. Right now, do this exercise:

- *As each thought forms in your mind, describe it by saying to yourself, "I am having the thought that . . ."*

■ *Keep going until you begin to feel a little detached from your thinking and the thoughts themselves seem slightly less important.*

Use this exercise whenever you're troubled by worries or self-judgment, and you need a little perspective.

Remember—thoughts aren't identity; they aren't reality. They're no-thing. They are just . . . thoughts.

— 31 —

the fishing boats

◆

imagine that you are on a bridge overlooking a harbor. Behind you is the open sea; before you a narrow channel is bordered by wharfs and gaily painted buildings. Further up channel, it broadens, and you can see in the distance many small docks. Some are empty; some hold fishing boats with their high twin poles used for casting nets.

It's dawn. In the half-light the boats are starting to head for the sea. A ragged procession of fishing craft is sputtering down channel, and passing under your bridge. Some are larger, some narrow and fragile looking. Some are wooden with peeling blue paint, some are a bright white, and some are metal with gun-colored hulls.

As the boats approach, single file, you can see them sway slightly. The windows of their cabins catch the early light and flash bright orange for a moment.

These boats are your thoughts, coming one after the other. Some are bigger and brighter than others. Some you hardly notice before they pass beneath you on the bridge. Though some may catch your eye and your attention, they're just a string of thoughts with none more important than the other. They appear, are briefly noticed, and pass out of sight. Watch your thoughts move, like the painted boats, slowly but inevitably out of awareness. As soon as one is gone, another boat or another thought takes its place. And then it, too, is gone. No more significant, no more important than any other.

You let them pass beneath you—and go. One at a time, briefly watching and letting them disappear. The sun is coming up, glinting off the ripples and the wakes. It warms you.

— 32 —

letting go of judgments

many carnivals and county fairs have an attraction called Pitch-and-Dunk. A man sits on a narrow seat above a tank of cold water. He hurls insults at the crowd, who, in turn, buy the right to pitch three baseballs at a target. If a ball hits the target, Big Mouth's seat collapses and he's dunked. Our judgment thoughts are like that—the more we aim them at others, the more likely they are to turn around and give us a cold dunking.

It's time to learn how to use mindfulness to free yourself from the power of judgment. We'll start by focusing on your judgments about others, and then work on self-attacks.

To begin, bring your attention to your breath. Observe the feeling of the cool air in your throat, the rise and fall of your chest, the stretching of your diaphragm, and the release as you exhale.

Now visualize a person you don't like. Form a clear impression of their face and posture; try to hear the person's voice. As judgmental thoughts take shape in your mind, notice and then let them go. Put each thought on a leaf floating down a stream. Watch as it drifts around the bend and out of sight. Do the same with the next thought and the next. Keep this up for at least three minutes.

Refocus on your breathing. Now visualize a recent event in which you were upset and someone behaved in a way that felt wrong, dangerous, or foolish. Get a clear mental picture of what happened and what was said. Again, as judgmental thoughts rise in your mind, watch briefly and let go of them. Let them float away on a leaf and out of sight.

Return your attention to your breath. Now imagine yourself standing naked in the mirror. Visualize a part of your body that you don't like. Listen for judgments, and don't get caught in them. Put them on the leaf and let them drift out of sight.

One last time, attend to your breath. Now create a mental image of something you once did but now regret. As the scene comes into focus, and you watch the event unfold, notice your thoughts. Then place each thought on a leaf and let it go.

If you like how mindfulness helps you feel during storms of judgment, we encourage you to do this exercise each time you catch yourself playing Pitch-and-Dunk.

— 33 —

draw your thoughts

imagine one of your scary thoughts turned into a big gorilla hulking over a thimble-sized version of you. How would picturing a thought that way change your relationship to it? This exercise—turning thoughts into pictures—is a way to soften the impact of your thoughts and give yourself a bit more distance from them.

Right now, we'd like you to recall several thoughts you've had in the last week or two that had some emotional punch. Select:

■   *A thought that scared you.*

- *A thought that made you feel bad about yourself (unworthy, ashamed, guilty).*

- *A thought that irritated you.*

Write each thought down at the top of a separate piece of paper. Now draw the thought. If you have any, use crayons or colored pencils. Otherwise, black or blue ink is fine.

When drawing a thought, you could turn it into an animal, a locomotive, a tree, a whining baby, an angry old man shaking his cane, a snow-capped mountain, your mother, a crashing wave, a big pile of cumulus, railroad tracks converging toward the horizon, a merry-go-round, a broken doll, or anything. You're looking for a metaphor—an object that represents some aspect of your thought. It could reflect the power or persistence of the thought, its size, or where it comes from. It could represent its depth or arbitrariness. Have fun with this. Be creative.

Now consider doing one more thing with the picture. You might try adding yourself. How big are you relative to the thought? How close or far away are you? Are you turning your back, embracing it, or being enveloped by the thought?

If you've added yourself to the picture, here's a question: Is this where you want to be relative to the thought? Would you like to be bigger? Stronger? Farther away? Go ahead and redraw the picture with yourself at the size and distance you want to be.

— 34 —

say it again, sam

We all have thoughts that thunder into our minds like a runaway train. Big, heavy, irresistible.

- *I'm stupid (or ugly, or a loser).*

- *I'm losing my job.*

- *I screwed up.*

- *She doesn't care about me.*

We never question them because they seem so true and right; they seem to fit so neatly into what we've always believed. We just get run over by them. Cognitive scientists call them *automatic thoughts* because these show up with a will of their own. They leave a wake of shame, fear, or defeat.

One amazingly simple way to reduce the power of automatic thoughts is to repeat them. Out loud. It's called Titchener's Repetition, and it's based on the discovery that if we just keep saying something—about fifty to one hundred times—it loses all meaning and the power to hurt us. No matter how menacing the thought is when you start, it becomes absurd or silly as you keep saying it.

Okay, let's do it and see what happens. Sometime in the last hour you had a thought that bothered you. It might have been a "what if" worry, or something that made you feel bad about yourself. Whatever it was, reduce it to one or two words, and say them out loud right now. Keep saying them at least fifty times or until you stop feeling anything about them. Sooner or later, they will lose their power because they will lose all significance. They will become mere words; nothing you have to buy or believe.

Notice that part of the power of automatic thoughts lies in their secrecy and in your effort to avoid them. When you do the exact opposite by saying a thought often and out loud, it becomes no more important than an oft-heard commercial on the radio. They become words so boring and mundane, you've stopped listening.

songs and silly voices

imagine if you sang your critical, self-attacking thoughts to the tune of "Happy Birthday."

I am a big fool,

I am a big fool,

I *am* a big fo-ol,

And an i-di-ot too.

Suppose you kept singing it till the words lost all sting, till "fool" and "idiot" seemed no more hurtful than words like "travel" or "rhododendron."

Do it now. Take the last upsetting thing your mind said and put it to music. Use some familiar—even silly—

tune and turn your thoughts into lyrics. Let's take "Home on the Range," for example:

> Why, why do I fail
>
> while my friends and ex-lovers succeed?

Or the Beatles' "Yesterday":

> Every day, all I ever do is make mistakes.
>
> There's disaster hanging over me . . .

Or "Row Your Boat":

> Screw, screw, screw it up
>
> Every single day.
>
> Hate my job, hate my job, hate my job,
>
> Hate my job—
>
> But I have to stay.

Or "Frère Jacques":

> I am stupid.
>
> I am stupid.
>
> Can you see?
>
> Can you see?

The idea is to put some of your persecutory thoughts into a different context. As songs, they can take on a mocking, light-hearted tone. Instead of feeling so important and true, they begin to seem a little absurd and a bit over-done.

Another fun way to look at your painful thoughts from a distance is to say them with silly voices.

- *Try talking like Donald Duck to describe one of your flaws.*

- *Or be Blanche DuBois—"Ah have always destroyed every chance that was given to me."*

- *Or use a newscaster voice—"At one of San Francisco's largest department stores, _____ (your name) bought something useless and overpriced today."*

- *Or be a "damsel in distress," describing something you worry about. "Oh no (in a high-pitched voice), I'm never going to . . ."*

No matter how sharp or harsh your thoughts might be, songs and silly voices are a great way to soften them.

the thought scramble

ever played a word scramble in the newspaper? This exercise requires a piece of paper and pen. We're going to play a word scramble. What do the letters below spell?

R F E A

Did you get it? It spells "fear." We just took the letters from the word, put them in a different order, and suddenly, we took the fear out of fear. Now recall a fear thought you might have, such as, "I'm scared to go in an elevator." Write it down, first as a normal sentence. Notice how the "fear" emotion you have is actually a series of words. When you get close to the elevator, your heart races, and you think the same words in this order.

Now, write down the same sentence completely out of order. It might look like, "Go an I'm scared elevator in to." Say this new sentence to yourself ten times in a row. Does the scrambled sentence elicit fear in you? Now, write a scramble for a situation you fear. Keep the scramble in your wallet. Next time you approach something with that fear, take out your scramble, and say it to yourself, replacing your actual fear sentence. What happens to the meaning of the words when you do that? And what happens to your fear when you do that?

— 37 —

the paperweight

Some thoughts can press on your mind like a paperweight. They have the effect of holding you down. Some will make you feel physically heavy, perhaps even a bit dark and moody. These kinds of thoughts may come up in your mind as statements like, "Why me?" Or, " I don't know if I can handle this!" Thoughts about responsibility can feel like this, as can an illness we have to endure. There could very well be issues you are facing that bring on the heavy thoughts that weigh down all others. The papers beneath the weight may even have positive content. Why not just look underneath the weight, let out all that is there, and watch it all without taking sides?

Find a quiet place where you can sit quietly for at least five minutes. Consider specific thoughts in which the contents carry a certain amount of heaviness. Visualize that thought as a paperweight such as a large crystal, or a dark stone like a piece of granite. You don't need to lift the paperweight or remove it. All you need to do is realize that certain thoughts carry this kind of gravity. But just let them be what they are—paperweights. So, say to yourself, "I'm having the thought that I'm sort of down at the moment." Just notice the thought, and accept that it is present in your mind.

Now, also consider something that is important to you, something that exists alongside the paperweight thought. For instance, "I want to spend some time with my daughter tonight, maybe read a book to her after dinner." Visualize the action you'd like to take. Choose a time and place that you want to take the action, and allow that to guide what you decide to do with your time at some point in the day or night. Remember that paperweight thoughts can rest heavily on your mind, but you can still take action to do what matters to you, not by removing the paperweight, but by being aware of its existence and taking action anyway.

— 38 —

pop-up thoughts

most of us have had the experience of having really excellent, center row seats at a play, concert, or dance performance. You are excited all week and looking forward to the experience. Then, you're there, sitting close to the stage, and eager for the talent to take form before your eyes. The curtain rises, and the music begins. Within five minutes, your mind is roaming and jumping from thought to thought like a Mexican jumping bean. You worry and think, "Did I turn off the stove?" You plan for tomorrow, "First, I'll go for a run; and then I'll get breakfast going. Before I leave for work, I can quickly log on and pay the bills." Then, "Jesus! I'm here at the theater. I want to be here, now."

Sometimes your mind is mindless. It wanders, and it arrives at thoughts you don't even want to be having. You think you just want to pay attention and enjoy the show, and then you realize there are pop-up thoughts just like those pop-up ads on the Internet. Fine, let the thought pop up, and then, catch the fact that your mind is producing the thoughts. Watch the thoughts coming, fast, and let them be there. You decide whether or not to read what's in each window. Don't get involved with them. Just remind yourself you're having pop-up thoughts, an automatic stream of consciousness. You don't have to read them. Just recognize them for what they are, and click back on the performance.

— 39 —

well of sorrow

Life throws a lot at us. From the moment at birth when they slap us on the bottom all the way to the last medical procedures to sustain our lives, we have to deal with pain. Life is full of sadness, hurt, shame, fear, and loss. On top of all the unavoidable pain, we often end up heaping more on ourselves with our thoughts. We endure hard times, and then flog ourselves with judgments for what we did wrong. Or we speculate about what bad things might happen in the future.

It's as if the ordinary pain of life were not enough. We have to think about it, evaluate it, and make sense of it. And all that thinking seems to do one thing—turn our necessary, inescapable struggles into a deeper kind of suffering. We end up dealing with far more than our original loss or fear, because our thoughts act as a psychological bullhorn. They amplify and repeat everything. They keep blaring that we're stupid and no good, or create nightmare scenarios of what might befall us.

Here's something to consider: While the pain of life must be accepted, the add-on suffering caused by our thoughts is not necessary. What if our thoughts were nothing more than drops falling into a well of sorrow? What if our thoughts were momentary—forming and falling into the darkness, sensed only briefly before we let them go?

Do this exercise:

- *Observe your thoughts. Notice each one as it forms and takes shape.*

- *Then let it fall into the well of sorrow. Hear the tiny splash as each thought hits the water far below and disappears.*

- *It's a three-step process: notice, hear the splash, and let go. Do that for a few minutes and observe how your relationship to your thoughts changes. Do they still seem as important, as powerful? Do they have the same influence on your emotional life?*

white room meditation

Imagine you are in a medium-sized white room. There are no furnishings or decorations of any kind—just the bare walls. There's an open front door and open back door to the room, and darkness beyond the doors.

You can position yourself anywhere—floating in a corner or up near the ceiling. In a moment, with a little patience, the white room can become a place where you will learn to accept your mind.

Now imagine that your thoughts are entering the room. They come in from the darkness beyond the front door, one at a time, and leave by the back. Give each thought an image. You might start by visualizing them as bulked up

Mafiosi in Stetsons and overcoats. Then try other images. For instance, make your thoughts into:

- *Somersaulting circus clowns*

- *Walking broomsticks (like in* Fantasia*)*

- *Flying crows*

- *Stuffed shirts in a row*

- *Seals rocking along on their flippers*

- *Dancing razor blades*

- *Waddling penguins*

When you get bored with one image, move to another. As soon as a new thought enters your mind, bring in a new Mafioso or broomstick or crow through the front door.

Now here's something important: As each thought presents itself, neither resists nor get attached to it. Let it make its way through the room and out the back where it disappears in the darkness. Be a mere witness—sometimes laughing and never judging. Just observe until the individual thoughts begin to lose their importance, and you feel a growing detachment from them. In the white room you can accept your thoughts for what they are—creatures of the mind that live the briefest life and disappear.

take your chihuahua
for a walk

everyone knows what Chihuahuas do—they bark. Their instinct in life is to yap. They yap when the mailman walks by, they yap when you come home, and they even yap when no one is around and all is quiet. Sometimes they are silent, and who knows why they sometimes choose to just sit and watch a squirrel run by without making a peep.

Imagine your mind is like the Chihuahua. Thoughts can enter at random, with no notice, or sometimes without obvious provocation. Out of the blue, a thought enters your mind, and the next thing you know, your body reacts, perhaps with some fear or excitement. That's all it takes—a thought fires, and you react. Now, imagine that your mind is just like the small, yapping dog. Imagine that your thoughts are just like the barking that may have no cause, and are simply noises that pop out at random times.

Today, you are going to take the Chihuahua for walk. Sit still in a quiet room for even just five minutes. Imagine yourself clicking on his leash and stepping outside to take him for a short stroll. Each time a thought enters your mind, focus on the image of the Chihuahua barking. Maybe he is barking at a cat running across the street. Perhaps a butterfly landed in the grass near you both. He lets out a loud yap. Now a person walks toward you, and the dog goes nuts, jumping up and down and really barking at this person. The person passes, he forgets the person existed, and he's quiet again. Just let the dog bark for whatever reason, and then watch how he stops. He barks, and then he walks for a few moments in silence.

Each time a thought enters your mind, imagine it's just a bark. Some last longer than others, some are quick and high pitched, and some may growl and cower. Then the yapping stops as you keep walking and passing random objects that may or may not cause a reaction. You can observe your thoughts the same way you can imagine watching the Chihuahua. Thoughts are similar to barking—they may or may not have a cause or purpose. They come; they go. Watch them come, and then watch them go.

— 42 —

the unhappy customer

have you ever had to thank a customer for negative feedback? If you've ever worked in the service industry, most likely you've had this experience. You just nod, and thank the customer for their input.

Sometimes a negative thought or feeling is just like an irate customer. At times you have thoughts that, like unhappy customers, just complain, hate the food, hate the color, or hate the price, and so on. The unhappy customer wants to send the meal back, and let you know how responsible you are for his/her unhappiness.

Fortunately, that customer will eventually go away. Thoughts that bring these kinds of unpleasant experiences will also just come, and then leave the premises. You can note what the chief complaint is, but don't evaluate it, or decide if they're right or wrong. Your job is just to listen to their gripe, validate their experience, and help figure out what they'd like instead. Irate customers don't have to like everything, and you don't have to change their minds. All you have to do is listen and move on.

Remember, the thought belongs to the unhappy customer, not to you. Luckily, you can choose to notice the complaint, acknowledge the unhappiness, and then move on to the next table.

the thought lunchbox

What if thoughts were just like lunch in a lunchbox? You carry thoughts around the way a child carries around her sandwich in a lunchbox. The thoughts are in there, and you're carrying them around with you just as you would a bag of Fritos, an apple, and a juice box. A thought is often something you are lugging around. The key is that you don't have to eat or digest the thought. Just imagine certain thoughts as the contents of your lunchbox. Who cares if there's a liver sandwich in your lunchbox? You can just leave it in there and carry it around. You don't have to devour it.

To experiment with this idea, try carrying around your "liver sandwich" ideas on little pieces of paper or a few index cards.

- *Choose three nagging thoughts to ruminate. These are thoughts that seem to take over who you are. Thoughts of dread can be like that. For example, you're doing fine, and then you think, "I don't want to write my paper!" Or, "How am I ever going to get everything done?" Panic sets in, and then perhaps a sense of avoidance or a sense of paralysis. The thought hovers in your mind, scaring the dickens out of you.*

- *Write down each of these thoughts on a small piece of paper.*

- *Carry the pieces of paper around with you for an entire day.*

- *What does it feel like to carry your thoughts around with you as objects? Notice during the day whether you can just have them with you without getting involved and without arguing, agreeing, or disagreeing with them. Just have them with you.*

- *At the end of the day, ask yourself, "Was that okay? Can I do this with all my thoughts?"*

Each thought is just a thought, one that will come, and then, before you know it, a different one will appear. So why eat a liver sandwich? Try the lunchbox experiment with thoughts that aren't helping you get closer to what you actually need to do. Carry them around with you as objects.

— 44 —

hold a thought like a feather

What if you could hold a thought gently, as if it were as light as a feather? Imagine that you could hold a thought—any thought you struggle with—and just observe it, as if it were entirely new. Observe it with the curiosity of a child who is just learning to recognize the letters of the alphabet or petting a new kitten. Admire the thought with a sense of awe. Again, it can be any thought, such as:

"I'm having the thought that I'm anxious."

"I'm having the thought that I'm embarrassed."

"I'm having a thought that I'm sad."

At first, you might respond by clinging to the thought, or else battling it and trying to stamp it out of your mind. But today, in this moment, recall a thought with which you struggle regularly. Hold the thought in your mind, and hold it as lightly as a feather, as if the slightest breeze could come along and carry it away in the wind. Bring the thought to mind with fascination at how creative your mind can be in its efforts to assess the world. You may even laugh at how hard your mind works at holding onto this thought. Release the power it holds over you by visualizing it as a soft, white feather.

What does this thought do to serve you? Does it help you get closer to the people you love, or does it offer your body nutrients and longevity? Does it help you achieve what matters most to you? Just notice this thought with acceptance and compassion. Thank your mind for the thought, but realize you don't have to do anything with it or because of it.

— 45 —

the chocolate thought

a thought you try not to have rules your direction. Have you ever tried to diet? Tried *not* to think about chocolate, for instance, though it may be your favorite thing in the world? What happens when you *try not* to think about chocolate? Suddenly, it's all you can think about. As you attempt to stop it, control it, or eliminate the thought, it can soon dominate your experience. Now who's in control—you, or the chocolate thought?

We all have temptations, cravings, and the desire for instant gratification. You can learn to ride these thoughts out, to acknowledge that you have them and that you don't have to allow the chocolate thought to drive you in a direction you don't want to be going.

The key is acceptance. This entails becoming aware of the thought, and actively embracing the content of the thought. Chocolate pops into your mind. You can picture it, imagine where it might be hiding in your house, and even salivate a little just thinking about it. Now, focus on embracing the thought, and thank your mind for sending you the thought. In essence, don't try *not* to think the thought. What is more valuable to you? Acting on the chocolate thought? Or, do you value the ability to refrain, to sit with the craving but to ride it out? It will pass; all thoughts do. Instead, you might choose to select something that is healthy and that will bring a sense of comfort and wholesomeness, like a cup of tea, or some almonds and raisins. You've accepted the thought and chosen to direct your own actions.

— 46 —

feeding the tiger

Consider the plight of a man who owned a baby tiger. Even though the animal was small, it would growl in a frightening way and demand to be fed. The man was a bit unnerved by the tiger's ferocity, and immediately gave it a large portion of meat.

It placated the tiger for a little while, but the food also helped the tiger grow bigger. Each day when the tiger growled and threatened, the man ran to get it meat. The more the tiger growled, the more the man fed it, and the bigger and scarier and more dangerous the tiger became.

One day, when the tiger was long and strong and had claws like daggers, the man ran out of food. The tiger's growl was deep and menacing, but the man had already given it everything. The tiger didn't mind; the man would be a tasty meal.

Your scary, fortune-telling thoughts are like the tiger. The more they frighten you, the more you feed them by giving in and doing what they say. And the more you feed them, the stronger and scarier they get.

Think about it a moment. What do you do when a scary thought tells you to avoid something? Sometimes you give in and steer clear of what frightens you. Your mind tells you to stay home because you might feel awkward or embarrassed at a social gathering. Or your mind says you'll fail if you try to change jobs. So you hesitate. Or your mind suggests that your husband will get angry if you bring up a certain issue. So you stay quiet.

Every time you obey scary, fortune-telling thoughts by avoiding something worth doing, *you make your fears more powerful*. And eventually the fear tiger gets so big, it begins to consume your life.

When scary, fortune-telling thoughts well up, ask yourself:

■ *What is my mind trying to keep me from doing?*

- *If I listen to my mind, what valued goal or experience would I forego? What would I miss out on that matters to me?*

- *Am I willing to face this fear in order to do something worth doing? Or this time, will I listen to my scary thoughts and feed the tiger?*

letting worry
pass you by

What makes worry thoughts so powerful is that we embrace and resist them at the same time. We often embrace worry out of a belief that it might protect us. We think, "If I worry about it, it won't happen." It's as if worry were a good luck charm, a talisman that could keep us from harm.

On the other hand, worry thoughts are disturbing, and there is a natural impulse to suppress them. We try to push worry to the back of our mind where it boils and bubbles, forming a constant undertone of danger. It seems the more we push worry away, the more it inhabits our unconscious and darkens our sense of the future.

Changing your relationship to worry requires that you learn to neither embrace nor resist scary thoughts. Instead you will watch them as a sailor watches the waves of the sea—without particular meaning, without particular interest. Each wave is a small event followed by another. Each wave is a moment that passes.

Here's how to let worry thoughts pass you by:

- *First, and most important, notice them. Don't numb yourself or push them away.*

- *Right now, identify a recent worry. Let the thought take shape in your mind.*

- *Bring your attention to your breath. Feel it pass your throat and your trachea. Notice what the air feels like spilling into your lungs. Feel it push open your ribs and diaphragm. Feel the release as you begin to exhale.*

- *Notice what happens to your worry. Let it evolve and change. Let it begin its transformation to the next thought.*

- *Return to your breath. Feel it settle into your chest. Feel it fill and press open your ribs.*

- *Notice your thoughts again. Watch and let them pass.*

- *Get back to your breath. Take it in; let it go.*

- *Notice the next thought, something your mind has made up. Watch it pass and morph into another thought.*

- *Get back to your breath. Feel it make its way into your lungs and out again.*

- *Keep shifting between breath and thought until each thought is just a wave. And you are a sailor—fully alive, taking deep breaths—watching the waves pass you by.*

— 48 —

moving into your life

Sometimes you hold onto a thought as if your life depended on it, like a small child holding on tightly to her mother's skirt. The child holds on because she is so scared of going to school alone. Just the thought of it terrifies her, and she won't let go of what feels safe. But it's never the act of clinging to the pant leg that truly relieves the child of her fear. It's learning to let go, entering into the classroom, and doing whatever it was she thought she was afraid to do. What truly frees her from fear is *having the fear* and experiencing something anyway. It's natural to create ideas, thoughts, and desires that seem to keep you safe from what your past has taught you might harm you. As a consequence, you build up these safety thoughts, and you avoid experiences that your thoughts tell you might hurt you in some way.

While your mind tells you that holding on to the thought that keeps you safe will protect you, instead holding on to a thought is what binds you to suffering. For instance, you might think, "If I really feel the deep sadness within me, I might be so overwhelmed by it that I won't ever get up and function again." You don't want to experience sadness, so you resist experiences that may bring on sadness, like sharing intimacy with someone. You spend a lot of time keeping others at a distance, as you refuse to experience sadness. The safety thought is, "Don't get too close, and you won't feel sadness." You soon have a nice little moat built around you, with nice high walls that keep everyone out. So your thought succeeded in its first goal—to keep you from sadness. But now you have one pain on top of another—you have no intimacy, and yes, no sadness. But you might have a deeper thing—suffering.

Buddhists call the struggle to hold onto certain thoughts "clinging." Your mind becomes so narrowly focused on the one thought that keeps you from experiencing something you fear, that you become like the child clinging to the skirt, as if it protects you from pain. It's really more like avoiding a sensation that might feel uncomfortable. Sometimes allowing yourself to feel discomfort is more important, because your life is not restricted by a rule that you've created. When the child lets go, it's uncomfortable at first. But then, she moves forward into the classroom.

Today, choose a safe place to sit comfortably and consider just one thought you cling to. It could be a safety thought—something that you think you need in order to be safe emotionally, mentally, physically, or financially. Like, "I have to look good or no one will like me." Or, "If I don't have enough money, I'll never be secure." When you have that thought in mind, also ask yourself what else may be true beyond that thought. Like, "If I don't have enough money, I'll never be secure. And, I'll still be a kind and loving father."

Now try this:

- *Clench your fist tightly, as if you were holding onto the thought in the palm of your hand.*

- *Keep your fist tensed, clinging to the thought.*

- *Just notice if the rest of your body reacts to the thought with tension.*

- *Notice how the thought becomes the focal point of your awareness.*

- *Notice other thoughts that are stirred by this one.*

- *Take five deep breaths, each to the count of three.*

- *Relax your hand, opening the palm slowly to the count of three.*

Now try this:

- *Imagine a thought that goes beyond the original thought; one that might get you closer to something you value.*

- *Out loud, repeat your safety thought, followed by saying "and," and then name something that is also true for you.*

Whenever you recognize a thought as protective, say the thought out loud with an "and" thought following up. Become aware of the possibilities that lie beyond a safety thought.

— 49 —

dropping the rope

have you ever noticed how easy it is to give a good friend advice? She feels terrible about herself for some reason, and you sit and offer lots of great examples of how what she believes really isn't true. You spend a good amount of time convincing her that objectively, she is in fact smart, beautiful, and desirable.

You walk away content, but she isn't convinced for long. It's quite difficult, if not impossible, to talk our way out of feeling something. Just like getting drunk over a breakup numbs the pain temporarily, arguing with your thoughts can act as a short-term solution. Struggling with negative thoughts about yourself, such as "I'm never good enough," or

"No one will ever love me," by trying to talk yourself out of those thoughts, is arguing with yourself. You're arguing with your own painful thoughts and feelings, and it becomes like a game of tug-of-war. On one side you have the bad thoughts and feelings about yourself that compete with the thoughts on the other side of the rope that tell you, "You're not so bad! I've noticed people actually *do* like you!" This argument takes a tremendous amount of time and energy.

What if you just dropped the rope and ended the struggle? If you're willing to have the negative thoughts, you can accept them for what they are—thoughts. No thought or feeling is permanent. Just allow yourself to have the thought, because you know you will survive it. Survive it by *observing* the thought rather than just believing it as the end-all truth. Next, *choose* to respond to the thought by choosing an action that moves you in the direction of what you value and care most about in life. It takes practice and effort, but your quality of life will actually change. You will now notice that you are having a thought, and will remember to get into the seat of the witness and watch a thought without judging or changing it. That is what dropping the rope really means.

On a separate piece of paper, list three negative, self-evaluative thoughts with which you struggle. These are thoughts you have, but that you try to talk yourself out of, or try to escape in some way. Now imagine the thoughts in a game of tug-of-war, with opposing thoughts on either side of the rope. With each negative self-thought, ask yourself:

- *Am I willing to have this thought?*

- *Am I willing to practice mindfully observing this thought and allow it to be present?*

- *Do I want this thought to direct how I live my life?*

- *Am I ready to take action to expand the quality of my life?*

- *What does this thought stop me from doing?*

- *Am I willing to have this thought* and *do what I care about anyway?*

Mindfulness is a way to cherish what is happening now, and not what has happened, or what may happen. Your thought is happening now. If you're remembering something that was painful, shift your awareness back to the here and now. If you're dreading something in the future, come back to now. Notice where you are in this moment. Do some breath counting to the count of ten.

Drop the rope, choose an action based on what you want, and practice being mindful of the present moment.

monsters

Sometimes our thoughts are so scary, they're like monsters standing in front of us that keep us from moving where we want to go. They shout things like: "He'll leave you." "This is going to fail." "You don't know what you're doing." "Those people don't want you around." "You're ugly. Stay home." "You'll screw it up."

Notice that the effect of monster thoughts is to keep you stuck and paralyzed. They make it too frightening to do some of the things that really matter in your life. So what happens? You avoid decisions, situations, or people. You steer away from cherished goals. You numb yourself to the disappointment of living so differently than you'd hoped.

Here's something to consider that might begin to free you. Monster thoughts are just products of your mind. They aren't reality; they are mere fortune-telling. They offer a picture of the future—of what could happen and how you might feel—that may never occur. What if the monsters kept you from doing something very important, and they were nothing more than an idea or a scary image?

Here's a new way to relate to monster thoughts:

- *Imagine you are driving a bus. The bus is your life and the whole of what you are and want to be. You are trying to drive your bus in a direction that matters to you, or toward valued goals and desires. Right now identify at least one goal— something you really care about—that has felt too scary to pursue.*

- *Now try to visualize this goal. See yourself moving toward it. Hold the image until it's clear in your mind, and you start to notice some of the monster thoughts. "They'll laugh at me." "She'll get angry." "You'll be alone." "You'll run out of money." "You'll be too exhausted." Listen to the monsters, knowing they are just mental chatter, just ideas. Now write down each thought.*

- *Now imagine you are driving the bus toward your goal, and all the monster thoughts are right in front of you. They don't want you to get there. Give them faces, and hear them shouting and carrying on. You're stuck. The monsters are between you and where you want to go.*

- *There's only one thing you can do—invite the monsters on your bus. Open the door and let them in. Imagine each ugly face, full of vicious glee, coming up the steps and taking a seat behind you. They're all chattering their scary stuff and making a ruckus. It's hard to listen to them because they fill you with uncertainty, or just plain fear. But something important has happened. The monsters aren't in front of you anymore and blocking your way. You can drive the bus— your life—where you want to go. You can pursue that valued goal, as long as you are willing to take the monsters with you and listen to their shouts and warnings.*

This is what we do to live full, valued lives. We have to put up with monster thoughts, and do what matters anyway. Imagine that goal again—the one the monsters have made it hard to follow. What if you did it anyway and just took those nattering nabobs with you?

Matthew McKay, Ph.D., is a professor at the Wright Institute in Berkeley, CA. He is the author and coauthor of more than twenty-five books, including *The Relaxation and Stress Reduction Workbook, Messages, When Anger Hurts, Self-Esteem,* and *The Self-Esteem Guided Journal.* He received his Ph.D. in clinical psychology from the California School of Professional Psychology. In private practice, he specializes in the cognitive behavioral treatment of anxiety, anger, and depression.

Catharine Sutker is an editor and freelance writer living in the San Francisco Bay Area. She is the coauthor of *The Self-Esteem Companion, The Self-Esteem Guided Journal, and The Self-Nourishment Companion.*